# FACT ★ OR FAKE?

# THE TRUTH ABOUT
# SCIENCE

## ALEX WOOLF

First published in Great Britain in 2022 by Wayland
Copyright © Hodder and Stoughton Limited, 2022

Produced for Wayland by
White-Thomson Publishing Ltd
www.wtpub.co.uk

All rights reserved.

Editor: Alex Woolf
Series Designer: Rocket Design (East Anglia) Ltd
Consultant: Steve Parker

HB ISBN: 978 1 5263 1844 2
PB ISBN: 978 1 5263 1845 9

Wayland
An imprint of
Hachette Children's Group
Part of Hodder & Stoughton
Carmelite House
50 Victoria Embankment
London EC4Y 0DZ

An Hachette UK Company
www.hachettechildrens.co.

Printed in China

| WEST NORTHAMPTONSHIRE COUNCIL | |
|---|---|
| 60000518085 | |
| **Askews & Holts** | |
| | |
| BB | |

Picture acknowledgements:

Shutterstock: Vector.design cover, title page and 29, The Toon Company 3, zizi_mentos 4, Cory Thoman 5, Morphart Creation 6, PinkPeng 7l, Astarina 7r, Moriz 8, CloudyStock 10–11 and 92–93, siridhata 12, Marylia 14, Martian Red 15, Slice Lemon 17, musmellow 18, Zdenek Sasek 19, animicsgo 20, SpicyTruffel 21, ex_artist 22–23, dimair 24, GabrielJose 25, Natalya Levish 26, DeShoff 27, Gommy Icon Studio 28, Netkoff 29, M-vector 30, nickolai_self_taught 31 and 47t, Swill Klitch 32, CG_dmitriy 33, Sudowoodo 34–35, jehsomwang 36, Tupungato 37, lineartestpilot 38, Jane Rix 39, Yeti Crab 40, Visual Generation 41, bypty 43, N.D. Fernandez 44, BeRad 45, Maxim Cherednichenko 46, Golden Shrimp 47b, AntartStock 48, digitalmumi 49, H N Y 51, Fandorina Liza 52, Yayayoyo 53, Elvina Gafarova 53 (border), Catalyst Labs 54 and 95, Kachaya Thawansak 55, Lemonade Serenade 57, Dovgaliuk Igor 58, aksol 59, autumnn 61, NikomMaelao Production 62, derGriza 63, hancik 66, Sapunkele 67, mijatmijatovic 68, metamorworks 70, Visual Generation 71, Oleksandr Panasovskyi 72, Number 86 73, Iuliia Koneva 75, white whale 76, Artsem Vysotski 76 (background), dimpank 77, Christophe BOISSON 78, Giorgio Morara 79, Mona Monash 80, Alenka Karabanova 81, Zvigo17 82–83, Anatolir 83, Alexander_P 84l, MoreVector 84r, Complot 85, rudall30 86, OsherR 87, Andrio 89, Kate Macate 90, MoreVector 91.

All design elements from Shutterstock.

Every effort has been made to clear copyright. Should there be any inadvertent omission, please apply to the publisher for rectification.

The website addresses (URLs) included in this book were valid at the time of going to press. However, it is possible that contents or addresses may have changed since the publication of this book. No responsibility for any such changes can be accepted by either the author or the publisher.

All facts and statistics were correct at the time of press.

# CAN YOU SEPARATE THE FACTS FROM THE FAKES?

WATER CAN BOIL AND FREEZE AT THE SAME TIME!

**SERIOUSLY??**

PISTACHIO NUTS CAN SPONTANEOUSLY BURST INTO FLAME!

**NO WAY!**

ATOMS ARE 99.999999% EMPTY SPACE!

**WHAT??**

TELEPORTATION IS IMPOSSIBLE.

**WOW!**

(IS IT THOUGH?)

Read on and find out the reality behind popular myths and mindblowing truths about science. Explore some of the stranger corners of our universe and then dazzle your friends and family with these bizarre, hilarious and totally amazing science facts!

# EVERY SNOWFLAKE IS UNIQUE

Watching snowflakes fall in their countless numbers, you ask yourself: can each one really be unique? The answer is that some may be extremely similar, but there's almost no chance that two snowflakes will be identical.

## THE SCIENCE

A snowflake is an ice crystal. Each branch of a snowflake can spawn others in countless different arrangements. The tiniest changes in temperature and humidity as it falls to Earth can alter the crystal's formation. According to some scientists, there are twice as many possible arrangements of crystals as there are atoms in the universe. That's why it's incredibly unlikely that two snowflakes will be exactly the same.

**VERDICT**

## Fact

4

# BENJAMIN FRANKLIN DISCOVERED ELECTRICITY

## FACT OR FAKE?

American scientist Benjamin Franklin (1706–1790) greatly advanced our knowledge of electricity. He experimented with static electricity and showed how electricity flowed between positive and negative elements. However, it wouldn't be true to say Benjamin Franklin discovered electricity.

## THE SCIENCE

The English scientist William Gilbert studied this force more than a hundred years before Franklin, and the English writer Sir Thomas Browne gave us the word electricity in 1646.

### THE KITE IN THE STORM

Franklin showed that lightning was a form of electricity with a very dangerous experiment: he flew a kite in a thunderstorm. The kite's string, wetted by the rain, conducted electricity, causing a metal key attached to the string to spark.

VERDICT
**Fake**

# THERE ARE THREE STATES OF MATTER

What! So I don't MATTER now?

## FACT OR FAKE?

The three states of matter that we find most commonly on Earth are **solid, liquid** and **gas**. Others also exist, however. One is plasma. This is similar to a gas, but it has a positive electric charge. Stars such as the Sun are made of plasma.

## THE SCIENCE

Like gas, plasma has no fixed shape or volume. It's made up of ions – atoms that have had some or all of their electrons stripped away. This is what gives it a positive charge.

### SUPER-CHILLED MATTER

In 1995 scientists created a fifth state of matter. They cooled a substance down to such a low temperature that all the atoms started clumping together to make one "super atom".

**VERDICT**
............
**Fake**

# LIGHT AND RADIO WAVES ARE DIFFERENT FORMS OF THE SAME THING

## FACT OR FAKE?

The light we detect with our eyes, and the radio waves we pick up on a radio receiver, are both forms of radiation – energy that travels through the air in waves. The only difference between them is the length of the wave. Light waves have a shorter length than radio waves.

## THE SCIENCE

There are many different forms of radiation, including the microwaves you use to cook your popcorn and the X-rays that can see inside your body. Together, they make up the electromagnetic spectrum.

VERDICT

Fact

# EVERYTHING THAT MOVES WILL EVENTUALLY COME TO A STOP!

Wooah!

If you throw a ball, it moves in a straight line for a bit, then it comes back to the ground and stops. But this only happens because of forces acting on it, like gravity and friction. If you threw a ball in deep space it would keep moving in a straight line forever, or until some external force acted on it.

## THE SCIENCE

Scientists use the term inertia to describe this tendency for objects to keep moving unless acted on by another force. Inertia is why we need seatbelts. If a car crashes, the people inside will keep moving forward at the same speed unless they are held in place.

## VERDICT
**Fake**

# HEAT MAKES THINGS GROW

# BIGGER

## FACT OR FAKE?

Solids, liquids and gases all expand when they are heated. For example, thermometers work because the liquid inside them expands and rises up the tube when the temperature gets hotter.

## THE SCIENCE

When a substance is heated, its atoms vibrate faster, so the volume they take up expands. Liquids expand more than solids when heated because their molecules are less tightly bound. For the same reason, gases expand more than liquids.

## VERDICT
### Fact

### STUCK LID?

If you can't unscrew a lid from a glass jar, ask an adult to place it in hot water for a few seconds. The heat will cause the metal lid to expand, making it easier to unscrew.

# LIGHTNING

## NEVER STRIKES IN THE SAME PLACE

# TWICE

## FACT OR FAKE?

This is a phrase you've probably heard before. It's often used to reassure people that bad luck won't repeat itself. However, the truth is, lightning can and does strike in the same place twice.

### SKYSCRAPERS

Tall buildings are more likely to be hit by lightning during a storm, because they reduce the distance the lightning bolt needs to travel. The Empire State Building in New York City gets hit around 25 times a year.

## THE SCIENCE

Lightning is a discharge of electricity that has been building up in a cloud. It travels downwards until it reaches the ground. Lightning bolts strike at random, so there's nothing to stop the same place being hit twice.

VERDICT
**Fake**

# CRACK!

# THE CRACK OF A WHIP IS CAUSED BY IT BREAKING THE SOUND BARRIER

## FACT OR FAKE?

If you jerk a whip hard it makes a loud crack. The whip isn't hitting anything solid, so why does it make that sound? It's actually caused by part of the whip breaking the sound barrier, causing a "sonic boom".

## THE SCIENCE

Researchers have worked out that a whip's sonic boom comes from a loop travelling along the whip, gaining speed until it breaks the sound barrier.

### THE SOUND BARRIER

Sound moves at around 1,120 km/h through the air. If something moves faster than that, it creates shockwaves in the air, causing a crack or longer booming sound.

## VERDICT
## Fact

**THE DIRECTION WATER SWIRLS DOWN AND THE PLUGHOLE IS DIFFERENT IN THE NORTHERN AND SOUTHERN HEMISPHERES**

Many of us have heard that water swirls down the plughole clockwise in the southern hemisphere and anticlockwise in the northern hemisphere. This isn't true. It can swirl in either direction, wherever you are.

## THE SCIENCE

This myth is based on something called the Coriolis effect. The Earth's surface spins at different speeds, depending on where you are. At the poles it spins slowly and at the equator it spins fast. This influences the direction in which ocean currents and storm systems spin in each hemisphere. But the Coriolis effect is tiny at the scale of bathtubs, and too weak to affect the way water swirls down plugholes.

**VERDICT**

**Fake**

# A CLOUD CAN WEIGH AS MUCH AS 35 BUSES

## FACT OR FAKE?

We don't think of clouds as heavy because they float around in the sky. Yet clouds are made of a substance – water vapour – so they must have weight. Some of them weigh a great deal.

## THE SCIENCE

How can clouds float if they're heavy? The reason is that air itself also has weight. Since it has weight, it also has density. Clouds float because the moist air they are made of is less dense than the dry air beneath them.

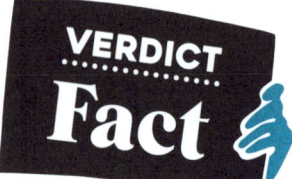

**VERDICT**
## Fact

### WEIGHING A CLOUD

A cloud with a volume of 1 cubic km weighs around 500,000 kilograms, or roughly 35 school buses.

# A PENNY DROPPED FROM THE EMPIRE STATE BUILDING CAN KILL A PERSON

There's a story that a penny dropped from the top of the Empire State Building would gather so much speed as it fell that it would kill someone standing below. In theory, an object dropped from this height would reach a speed of 103 km/h when it hit the ground, but a penny would never reach that speed because of its shape.

## THE SCIENCE

The flat surface of a penny causes the air to push up on it as it falls through the air, slowing its acceleration. So a penny falling from the Empire State Building would only hit the ground at 40 km/h. Because a penny is so light, this probably wouldn't cause anything worse than a bruise.

VERDICT
Fake

15

# GLASS IS ACTUALLY A LIQUID

## FACT OR FAKE?

In cathedral windows, glass is sometimes thicker at the bottom than at the top. It's as if the glass is a very slow-moving liquid that over the centuries has flowed downwards. Actually, glass isn't a liquid, but it's not a normal solid either.

## THE SCIENCE

Glass is a solid with some liquid properties. Unlike normal solids, glass has molecules that lack a regular structure and move around. Unlike liquids, the structure is quite rigid and the molecules only move very slowly. It would take billions of years for glass to flow even a tiny bit!

### CATHEDRAL GLASS

The glass in cathedrals is uneven because of the way it was made back in medieval times.

**VERDICT**
**Fake**

# SOME METALS EXPLODE WHEN THEY TOUCH WATER

Certain metals, known as alkali metals, react violently when they are placed in cold water. They may move around and fizz. Some even explode.

## THE SCIENCE

When alkali metals, such as lithium, sodium and potassium, react with water, they produce heat and give off hydrogen gas. The heat may ignite the hydrogen or the metal itself, causing a fire or an explosion.

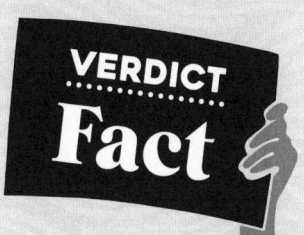

VERDICT
Fact

# OXYGEN HAS A COLOUR

## O₂

### FACT OR FAKE?

In its gas form, oxygen has no colour. Yet when in liquid form, oxygen is pale blue. As a solid, oxygen can be many different colours, including sky blue, orange and deep red.

### THE SCIENCE

When light hits an object, the object reflects back some of that light and absorbs the rest of it. Bananas, for example, reflect mainly yellow light. Liquid oxygen reflects blue light, hence its colour. Solid oxygen has different states (called phases), depending on the temperature and pressure. In each phase it reflects back a different colour.

### NORTHERN LIGHTS

The yellow and green colours of the Aurora Borealis, or Northern Lights, are caused by particles from the Sun colliding with oxygen and nitrogen in the atmosphere.

### VERDICT
## Fact

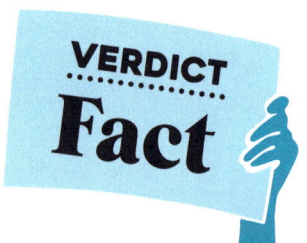

# A CAR IS HARDER TO MOVE THAN A BIKE BECAUSE IT WEIGHS MORE

Phew, this is heavy!

## FACT OR FAKE?

It's true that a heavy object is harder to move than a lighter object, but this is not because of its weight, it's because of the object's inertia (see pp8–9). The greater the weight of the object, the more inertia it has.

## THE SCIENCE

The inertia of an object is its resistance to a change in motion. Inertia makes it harder to move heavy things. It also makes it harder to stop heavy things once they're moving. So once you've got your car moving, you need a strong force to make it stop. That's why the brakes on a car have to be more powerful than those on a bike.

**VERDICT**
**Fake**

# HEAVIER OBJECTS FALL FASTER THAN LIGHTER ONES

## FACT OR FAKE?

If you drop two balls of the same size but one is heavier than the other, which will reach the ground first? Common sense might suggest the heavier one would. In fact, they'd both land at the same time.

## THE SCIENCE

Gravity acts on objects independently of their mass. In practice, the speed objects fall varies depending on their shape. The greater an object's surface area, the more air resistance it will encounter, slowing its fall.

### HAMMER AND FEATHER

There's no air resistance on the Moon, so when an astronaut on Apollo 15 dropped a hammer and a feather, they hit the ground at the same time.

**VERDICT**
## Fake

# IT TAKES JUST OVER 8 MINUTES FOR LIGHT TO TRAVEL THE SUN TO THE EARTH

## FACT OR FAKE?

The Sun that we see in the sky is 8 minutes and 20 seconds in the past. That's how long it takes for the Sun's light to reach us. Safety tip: never look directly at the Sun.

## THE SCIENCE

The Sun is around 150 million km from Earth. Light travels through the vacuum of space at almost 300,000 km per second. So it takes about 500 seconds to make the journey.

### VERDICT
## Fact

# LIQUID HELIUM

## FACT OR FAKE?

If you cool helium down to its liquid form, it will behave very differently from other fluids. It can dribble through cracks just a molecule wide, remain motionless when its container is spun, and flow up and over the sides of a dish.

## THE SCIENCE

What's going on? Helium atoms are extremely light and only weakly drawn to each other. This causes liquid helium to flow without friction, giving it these extremely weird properties.

# CAN FLOW UPWARDS

### SOLID HELIUM?

Helium has to be very cold to turn to liquid (−269 °C, or −452 °F) and it remains liquid at the lowest possible temperatures. Only under strong pressure does it become solid.

VERDICT
**Fact**

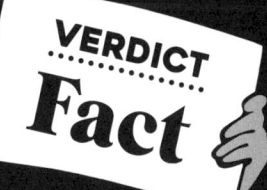

# TIME MOVES FASTER ON A MOUNTAIN THAN IT DOES AT SEA LEVEL

## FACT OR FAKE?

If you place a clock on top of a mountain and another on the beach, the beach clock will move very slightly more slowly. The differences will be tiny, but can be measured. This proves that time is not the same everywhere. It depends on where you are.

## THE SCIENCE

Time moves slower as you get closer to the Earth. This is because the gravity of a large mass, like a planet, warps the space and time around it. This effect is called time dilation, and it was discovered by the German-born physicist Albert Einstein.

### TINY DIFFERENCE

Scientists carried out an experiment to prove time dilation exists. They showed that a clock runs faster if it is raised by 30 cm, but the effect is tiny, losing just 90 billionths of a second over an average life span of 79 years.

VERDICT
Fact

# AN ATOM IS LIKE A MINIATURE SOLAR SYSTEM

When we look at pictures of atoms in old textbooks, they show little circles (electrons) going around a bigger circle (the nucleus). It looks a bit like a tiny solar system. This is wrong.

## THE SCIENCE

You can plot the movement of a planet and predict how it will move in future. You can't do that with an electron because, unlike a planet, you can never know for certain where an electron is. All we know is what energy they have and where we are likely to find them.

VERDICT
. . . . . . . . . .
**Fake**

# WATER CONDUCTS ELECTRICITY

## FACT OR FAKE?

We're always told not to mix water and electricity and that it's important to keep electrical appliances away from water – which is true. However, pure water is actually an excellent insulator and does not conduct electricity. To obtain pure water, you need to distill ordinary water by boiling it and then letting it condense in a clean container.

## THE SCIENCE

The water that falls as rain or comes out of our taps contains lots of dissolved substances, such as minerals and chemicals. These subtstances contain electrically charged particles called ions and they are what make water conduct electricity.

VERDICT
Fake

# LASERS CAN GET TRAPPED IN A WATERFALL

## FACT OR FAKE?

Lasers produce narrow, intense beams of light that can travel incredible distances in a straight line through the air. Yet it's possible to trap a laser beam in a stream of water.

## OPTICAL FIBRES

Fibre optic cables trap light beams in the same way. The light beams bounce repeatedly off the walls of the cable as they travel down it.

## THE SCIENCE

You can trap a laser beam in a waterfall by making a hole in a water-filled bottle so a stream of water flows out, then shining a laser through the bottle. If the laser hits the edge of the stream at a certain angle, it will reflect rather than pass through it, causing it to zigzag downwards inside the stream. This is because water is a denser medium than air.

**VERDICT**
## Fact

# MICROWAVE OVENS HEAT FOOD FROM THE INSIDE OUT

## FACT OR FAKE?

It's often said that microwave ovens cook from the inside out. This isn't true. They heat food from the outside in, just like other cooking devices.

## THE SCIENCE

Microwave ovens work by directing microwaves at the food. When they hit substances such as water, fats and sugars, they heat up the molecules. But if they hit something with very little liquid content, like a dry pie crust, the liquid inside the pie might heat up first. That's how the myth developed.

### ROTATING MOLECULES

Microwaves heat molecules by causing them to rotate. Molecules with positive and negative charges on opposite ends rotate to try and line themselves up with the electric field from the microwaves.

## VERDICT
### Fake

# THE AVERAGE ATOM IS ONE-TENTH OF A BILLIONTH OF A METRE ACROSS

## FACT OR FAKE?

Atoms are very, very small. A typical human hair is around a million atoms wide. A full-stop on a piece of paper contains around 5 million atoms. If an apple was magnified to the size of the Earth, then each of the atoms in the apple would be about the size of the original apple.

## THE SCIENCE

Atoms are the smallest particles of an element. Atoms of different elements vary in size. The largest atom (cesium) is roughly nine times bigger than the smallest (helium).

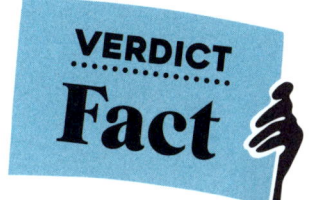

**VERDICT**
*Fact*

# WATER CAN BOIL AND FREEZE AT THE SAME TIME

## FACT OR FAKE?

It seems impossible that water could boil and freeze at the same time. Water usually freezes at a shivery 0 °C, and boils at a scalding 100 °C. And yet, if the conditions are right, it can happen. It's called the "triple point", when the gas, liquid and solid forms of water all occur together.

## THE SCIENCE

Water reaches its triple point at slightly above freezing (0.01 °C), but crucially this has to happen when the atmospheric pressure (the pressure caused by the weight of the air) is lowered to 0.006 atmospheres. That's six thousandths of Earth's atmospheric pressure at sea level.

VERDICT

Fact

# DIAMONDS
## ARE HIGHLY COMPRESSED
# COAL

## FACT OR FAKE?

Coal is formed from dead plant matter, changed over millions of years of heat and pressure into a brownish-black rock. Like diamond, it's made of carbon, but despite what some people might think, diamond is not highly compressed coal.

## THE SCIENCE

Most diamonds are much older than Earth's first land plants, the original material of coal. Diamonds require extremely high temperatures and pressures to form, conditions only found deep below Earth's crust in the mantle. The diamonds we mine formed in the mantle and were then pushed to the surface by volcanic eruptions.

### ASTEROID DIAMONDS

The extreme temperatures and pressures caused by an asteroid strike can sometimes cause diamonds to form on Earth's surface.

**VERDICT**
**Fake**

31

# GRAVITY IS A FORCE OF ATTRACTION BETWEEN TWO OBJECTS

## FACT OR FAKE?

We feel gravity as a force that holds us to the ground. But the physicist Albert Einstein showed that the gravity we feel is, in fact, a warping of space-time caused by the presence of a massive object – in our case, Earth.

## THE SCIENCE

If you imagine space-time as a rubber sheet, a massive object like Earth sitting on the sheet will warp it, causing you and everything else nearby to fall towards it.

**VERDICT**

**Fake**

## LIGHT AND GRAVITY

How do we know Einstein's right? If gravity was a force of attraction between objects, it wouldn't affect light, which has no mass. Yet the path of a beam of light is deflected by the warping effect of gravity.

# LIGHT CAN PUSH
## SPACECRAFT THROUGH SPACE

Spacecraft of the future could be powered by sunlight using solar sails. Once they've run out of fuel, the power of the Sun could keep them accelerating through their voyage, providing they don't travel too far from the solar system.

## THE SCIENCE

Light is made up of particles called photons. Photons have no mass, but they have momentum. As they hit the shiny solar sail, they reflect (bounce) off it and transfer their momentum to the sail, giving the spacecraft a push. Each push is tiny, but they add up, and each one slightly increases the spacecraft's speed.

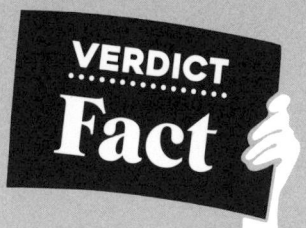

**VERDICT**
*Fact*

# BANANAS
## ARE
## RADIOACTIVE

It's true, they are – but only slightly. Bananas are rich in potassium, including a form of that element called potassium-40, which is radioactive. But you have nothing to fear from bananas because you're already far more radioactive than a banana.

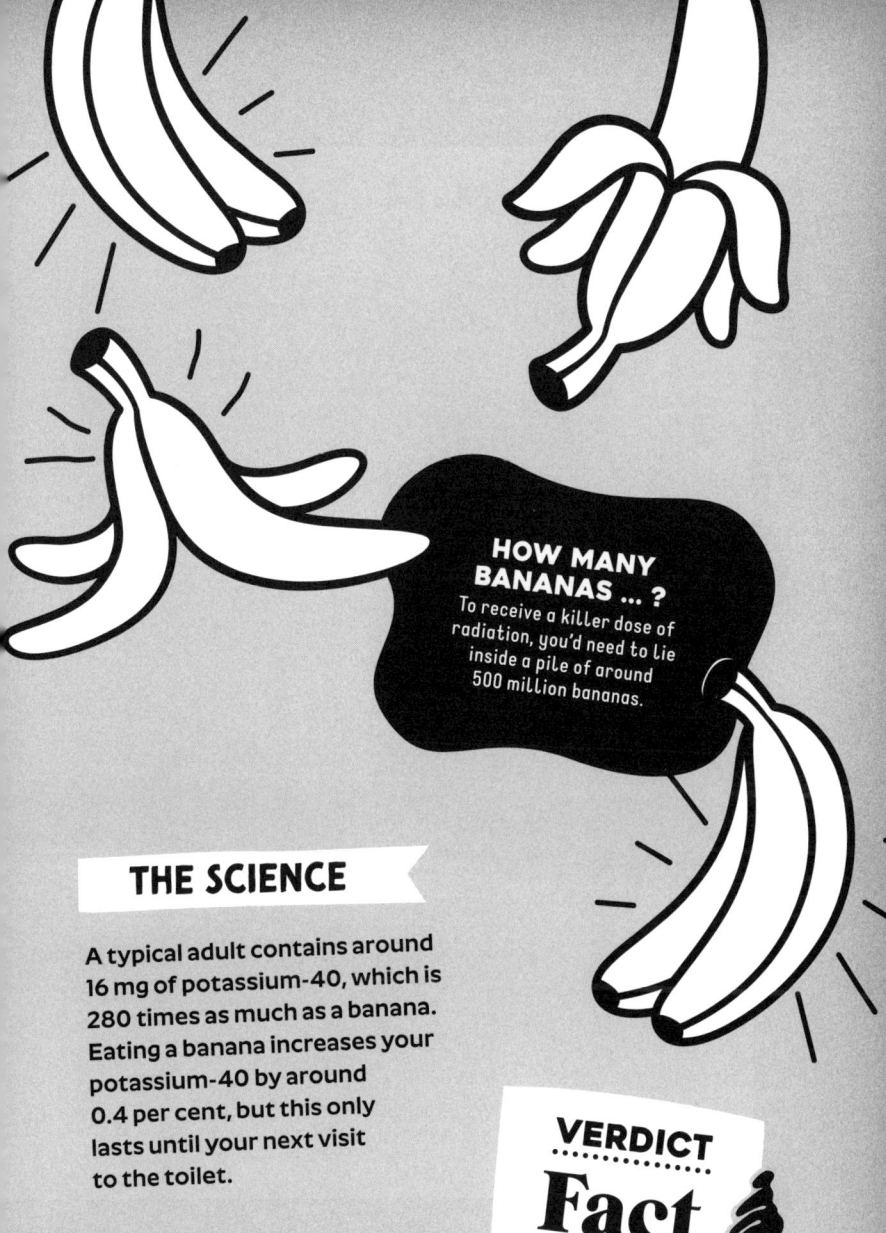

## HOW MANY BANANAS ... ?

To receive a killer dose of radiation, you'd need to lie inside a pile of around 500 million bananas.

## THE SCIENCE

A typical adult contains around 16 mg of potassium-40, which is 280 times as much as a banana. Eating a banana increases your potassium-40 by around 0.4 per cent, but this only lasts until your next visit to the toilet.

**VERDICT**

## Fact

# X-RAYS WERE DISCOVERED BY ACCIDENT

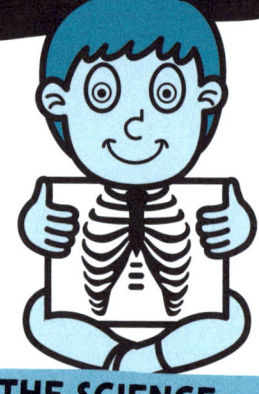

## FACT OR FAKE?

On 8 November 1895, German physicist Wilhelm Röntgen was experimenting with cathode rays (beams of electrons), generated by releasing an electric current in a special tube. He covered the tube with black cardboard and was surprised to see a green light escape and project onto a nearby screen. After experimenting, he found that this mysterious light would pass through most substances. He called it X-radiation.

## THE SCIENCE

X-rays are a form of electromagnetic radiation. They can penetrate soft tissue but not bone, so they allow doctors to create images of the bones inside our bodies.

**VERDICT**
*Fact*

# SPEED AND VELOCITY MEAN THE SAME THING

Dang, I'm going to get a velocity ticket!

CLICK

## FACT OR FAKE?

In everyday situations we think of speed and velocity as meaning the same thing. But for physicists, they have distinct meanings.

## THE SCIENCE

Speed refers to the time an object takes to cover a certain distance. Velocity is the time an object takes to change position. If an object moves very fast back and forth, it has high speed but zero velocity, because it hasn't changed position. To describe an object's velocity, you need to include information about its direction. The speed of an object might be 30 km/h, and its velocity might be 30 km/h east.

### ESCAPE VELOCITY

If you move in an upwards direction at 40,000 km/h, you've reached the speed needed to escape Earth's gravitational pull and will be able to reach space. This is known as escape velocity.

## VERDICT
# Fake

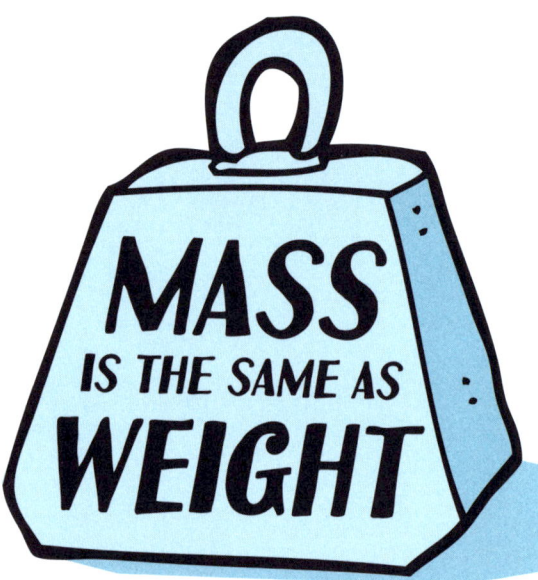

**MASS IS THE SAME AS WEIGHT**

We might think of an apple as weighing, say, 100 g, but this is the apple's mass, not its weight. We often mix up these two terms. This isn't a problem in ordinary life, but for a scientist there are important differences between the two forms of measurement.

## THE SCIENCE

Mass is the amount of matter in an object. Weight is the measure of the pull of gravity on the object. Mass is measured in kilograms. Weight is a force and it's measured in newtons (N). An apple with a mass of 100 g has a weight of 1 N.

**VERDICT**
**Fake**

# A METAL CAN BE LIQUID AT ROOM TEMPERATURE

## FACT OR FAKE?

We think of metals as solid at room temperature, and in almost all cases they are. However, there's one exception to this rule: mercury.

## THE SCIENCE

The electrons in a mercury atom are bound more tightly than usual to the nucleus, and it's reluctant to share them with other mercury atoms. As a result, the bonds between the atoms are relatively weak, and it takes very little heat for mercury to melt.

### MELTING METALS

Mercury is the only metal that's liquid at room temperature, but the metals gallium, caesium and rubidium melt at just a little warmer than that. You can melt gallium in the palm of your hand.

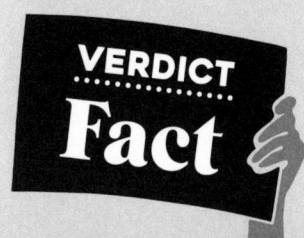

**VERDICT**
*Fact*

# ENERGY AND MATTER ARE THE SAME THING

## FACT OR FAKE?

In one of the most famous equations in history, E=mc2 (energy equals mass times the speed of light squared), Albert Einstein showed that energy and matter are different forms of the same thing. Matter is frozen energy, and energy is matter on the move.

## THE SCIENCE

With his equation, Einstein showed that the closer an object gets to the speed of light, the more mass it gains. In other words, part of the energy of the object's motion has transformed into matter.

### NUCLEAR POWER

Just as energy can be transformed into matter, so matter can be transformed into energy. We get nuclear power by converting some of the mass of atoms into energy.

**VERDICT**
## Fact

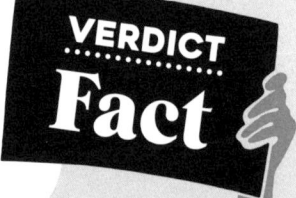

# TIME TRAVEL IS NOT POSSIBLE

CLONK!

WHIR!

## FACT OR FAKE?

We are all travelling through time at a rate of one second per second, but could we ever go faster than that and reach the future before other people? It sounds like science fiction, but it could be possible – in theory.

## THE SCIENCE

Albert Einstein proved that when we move through space we slow down the speed of our movement through time. This makes virtually no difference at normal speeds, but if we could get close to the speed of light, our personal clocks would run much slower than people on Earth's, so we could travel into Earth's future.

VERDICT

Fake

41

# WHITE LIGHT IS MADE UP OF ALL THE COLOURS OF THE RAINBOW

## FACT OR FAKE?

White light seems pure and empty of colour. In fact, it's made up of every colour of the rainbow – red, orange, yellow, green, blue, indigo and violet. A rainbow is formed when white sunlight is refracted off the inside of raindrops, and splits into its component colours.

## THE SCIENCE

Each colour of light has its own wavelength: red has the longest wavelength and violet has the shortest. When white light is shone at a raindrop (or a glass prism), it is refracted (the direction of the wavelengths is changed). Red light changes direction the least, violet light the most. That explains the order of colours we see in a rainbow.

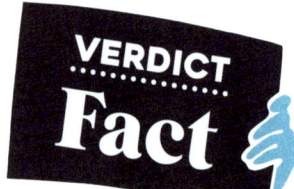

**VERDICT**
*Fact*

# YOU CAN'T FOLD A PIECE OF PAPER MORE THAN 7 TIMES

## FACT OR FAKE?

You'll struggle to fold an ordinary sheet of paper more than 7 times. However, with a big enough sheet and enough energy, there's no limit to the number of folds you can make.

## THE SCIENCE

The trouble is, with each fold you double the thickness of your paper. The average sheet of paper is 0.1 mm thick. After 10 folds, it'll be the thickness of a hand. After 23 folds, it'll be 1 km thick.

### KEEP FOLDING..

After 42 folds, it'll reach the Moon; 51 folds will get you to the Sun; if you manage 103 folds, your paper will be 93 billion light years thick – wider than the observable universe.

## VERDICT
## Fake

# AIR WEIGHS NOTHING

## FACT OR FAKE?

Air may not seem to weigh anything, yet it does. The only reason we don't notice it is because we're used to it. We know air has mass because you can feel it when the wind blows. On Earth (or anywhere else with gravity), something with mass also has weight.

## THE SCIENCE

At sea level, the total weight of the air above us exerts a pressure of a little over 1 kg per square cm. It exerts this pressure in all directions (up, down and sideways), which is why it doesn't crush us. Air weighs less at the top of a mountain, because there's less air above you.

### WEIGHING THE AIR

Air is weighed by measuring the pressure of the atmosphere. In 1643, Italian mathematician Evangelista Torricelli invented the barometer to measure atmospheric pressure.

## VERDICT
........
### Fake

# SPIN A BALL AS YOU DROP IT AND YOU CAN MAKE IT FLY

## FACT OR FAKE?

It seems to break the laws of physics, but you really can make a ball fly, if you drop it from a high place and give it a little spin first. This is called the Magnus Effect, named after German scientist Heinrich Magnus, who described it in 1852.

## THE SCIENCE

As the ball picks up speed, its spin pushes air one way and the air pushes on the ball the other way. This causes the falling ball to swoop and soar as it nears the ground.

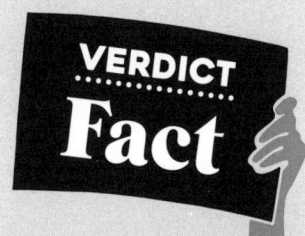

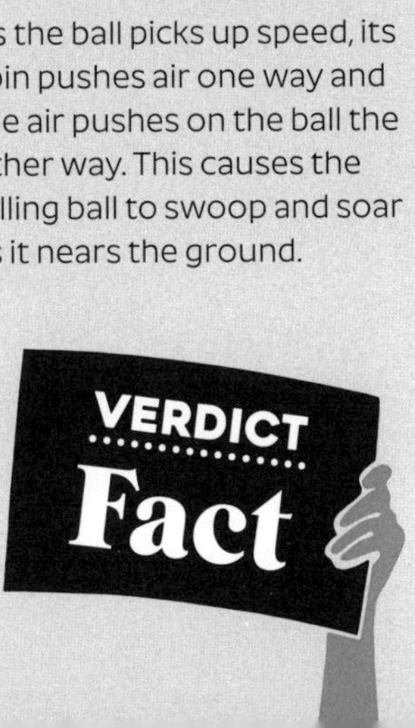

**VERDICT**
*Fact*

# THE GOLD WE MINE ON EARTH PROBABLY CAME FROM SPACE

## FACT OR FAKE?

Almost all of Earth's gold is trapped in its core where we can't reach it. The gold we mine probably came in meteorite and asteroid bombardments from space.

## THE SCIENCE

Gold is produced in violent cosmic events like collisions between stars. Energy from these collisions sent gold and other material flying into space where it was captured by other stars' gravity and eventually reached our planet in meteorites and asteroids.

## HOW MUCH GOLD?

There's enough gold in our planet to cover its entire land area with gold half a metre thick. Unfortunately, 99.5 per cent of it is in the core, where it can't be reached.

**VERDICT**

*Fact*

# DIAMONDS ARE THE HARDEST MATERIAL ON EARTH

## FACT OR FAKE?

Diamonds are famously hard, making them useful for drilling into dense rock. However, in recent years new materials have been created in the lab or found in nature that are even harder than diamond.

## THE SCIENCE

Diamonds are hard thanks to their rigid network of carbon atoms and the strong bonds between their molecules. The mineral lonsdaleite is also made from carbon atoms, but with a hexagonal crystal structure. Tests have shown lonsdaleite can withstand 58 per cent more stress than a diamond.

**VERDICT**
## Fake

47

# OBJECTS FLOAT BECAUSE THEY ARE LIGHTER THAN WATER

## FACT OR FAKE?

The reason objects float or sink isn't to do with their heaviness, but their density. That's why a heavy ship floats but a light coin sinks.

## THE SCIENCE

Density is a measure of how closely the molecules in a substance are squashed together. Metal sinks because it's denser than water. Wood floats because it's less dense. Steel ships float because the air inside them is less dense than water.

### SURFACE AREA

The more surface area an object has, the more water pushes back against it, so objects with a large surface area are better at floating – that's another reason why ships float.

**VERDICT**
............
**Fake**

# ELECTROMAGNETISM WAS DISCOVERED BY ACCIDENT

*Well I never!*

## FACT OR FAKE?

Until the early nineteenth century, scientists regarded electricity and magnetism as separate things. That changed on 21 April 1820 when Danish scientist Hans Christian Oersted made a startling discovery. During a lecture, he switched on an electric current, and the needle on his magnetic compass flickered. The audience didn't notice, but he did: he realised that electricity and magnetism were connected.

## THE SCIENCE

Oersted's discovery led scientists to realise that electricity and magnetism are both part of a single force called electromagnetism. This is why, if you pass electricity through a wire, it creates a magnetic field around the wire. Coil the wire around an iron bar and you create a temporary magnet called an electromagnet.

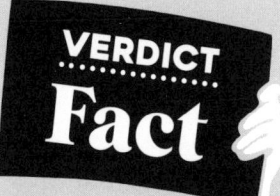

**VERDICT**
*Fact*

# LIGHT ALWAYS TRAVELS AT THE SAME SPEED

## FACT OR FAKE?

Scientists have calculated the speed of light at 300,000 km per second. But this is only its top speed – the speed it travels in a vacuum, such as space. Light travels at lower speeds when going through denser mediums, such as air or glass.

## THE SCIENCE

When photons (particles of light) travel through a dense medium, they are absorbed and emitted by particles along the way, which has a slowing effect. The denser the medium, the greater the slowdown.

**VERDICT**

## Fake

# A TYPICAL HURRICANE PRODUCES ENOUGH RAIN TO FILL 22 MILLION OLYMPIC SWIMMING POOLS

## FACT OR FAKE?

Hurricanes produce astonishing amounts of rainfall and energy. As well as filling all those swimming pools, the average hurricane generates 600 trillion watts of energy – equivalent to 200 times the electrical energy produced by all the world's power stations.

## THE SCIENCE

Only a quarter of 1 per cent of a hurricane's energy is its wind. The vast majority of its energy is in the form of heat stored and released as water vapour, which then falls as rain.

### CAPTURING HURRICANE ENERGY

Today's wind turbines are mostly too fragile to withstand a hurricane, but new designs, with vertical blades sandwiched between upper and lower platforms, could capture hurricane energy and convert it to electricity.

## VERDICT
### Fact

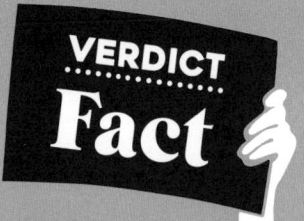

# PISTACHIO  NUTS

## CAN SPONTANEOUSLY BURST INTO FLAME

### FACT OR FAKE?

Pistachio nuts look harmless enough, and most of the time they are. But when stored in large quantities under the right conditions they sometimes heat up and even explode.

### THE SCIENCE

When stored in a damp atmosphere, such as a ship's hold, the nuts produce fatty acids. The pistachios take in oxygen and emit carbon dioxide, causing the fatty acids to break down. This process gives off heat, which can build and build until the nuts catch fire.

### SUFFOCATING NUTS!

As if threat of fire wasn't enough, pistachios pose another danger. If large amounts are stored in an enclosed space without ventilation, they can suck enough oxygen from the air to suffocate people.

**VERDICT**
**Fact**

52

# IT TAKES 24 HOURS FOR EARTH TO ROTATE ON ITS AXIS

## FACT OR FAKE?

There are 24 hours in a day and a day is the time it takes for Earth to rotate once on its axis, so surely it follows that Earth completes a rotation once every 24 hours. Not quite. It takes 23 hours and 56 minutes.

## THE SCIENCE

If each day is four minutes short of 24 hours, how come our dawns aren't getting ever earlier? The reason is that while Earth is rotating, it's also moving around the Sun, so for the Sun to reach the same point in the sky each day, Earth has to rotate one degree further. We don't measure days by Earth's rotation, but by the Sun's position in the sky.

### VERDICT
## Fake

# SOAP MAKES WATER WETTER

## FACT OR FAKE?

Water forms beads on your window because it has surface tension. Soap reduces water's surface tension so it spreads more easily, making it better at cleaning. This is often described as "making water wetter".

## THE SCIENCE

Most dirt contains oil, and oil and water don't mix, so water by itself isn't great at cleaning. Soap bridges this gap. The head of each soap molecule binds to water, breaking the surface tension. Meanwhile, the tail of the soap molecule binds to the dirt. When you rinse off the soap, the dirt goes with it.

### STRONG SURFACE

Water's surface tension is strong because the surface molecules are pulled tightly to the ones below, forming a skin. That's why some water bugs can skate across ponds.

### VERDICT

**Fact**

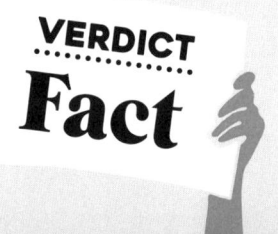

# A DUCK'S QUACK DOES NOT ECHO

Quack!

## FACT OR FAKE?

It's often been said that a duck's quack doesn't echo. This idea may have arisen because ducks tend to quack quietly and they live in open spaces far from buildings or mountains with large surfaces for sound to bounce off and produce an echo. In fact, it's a myth and scientists have proved this.

## THE SCIENCE

In 2003, a team of scientists placed a duck called Daisy in a special chamber and recorded her quacks. The team found that Daisy's long, fading quack masked the echo so it wasn't very audible, and that's maybe how the myth came about.

VERDICT

Fake

# MAGNETS ALWAYS HAVE TWO POLES, EVEN IF YOU CUT THEM IN HALF

| S | N | S | | N | S | N |

## FACT OR FAKE?

All magnets have two poles – north and south. If you cut a magnet in half, you'll end up with two magnets, each with a north and south pole. You could keep slicing a magnet into ever thinner pieces and end up with lots of thin magnets, each with two poles.

## THE SCIENCE

A magnet is actually a bundle of tiny magnets all squashed together, called magnetic domains. Each one strengthens the magnetic fields of the others. That's why you can cut a magnet into lots of smaller magnets. You must cut it gently, though. If you cut it roughly, the magnetic domains will be knocked out of alignment and no longer reinforce each other.

**VERDICT**

*Fact*

# THUNDER IS THE SOUND MADE BY LIGHTNING

## THE SCIENCE

As lightning strikes the ground, a second bolt of lightning returns from the ground to the sky following the same route as the first bolt. Heat from this rising bolt raises the temperature of the surrounding air to 27,000 °C. The heated air is first compressed and then explodes outwards. It's this that causes the sound of thunder.

## FACT OR FAKE?

We usually think of thunder as the sound made by lightning. However, the rumbling we hear is actually the noise of the air around the lightning bolt expanding.

### HOW CLOSE?

To work out how close lightning is, count the seconds between the lightning and thunder. Each second represents around 300 m.

**VERDICT**
......
**Fake**

57

# NOTHING CAN MOVE FASTER THAN LIGHT

Don't blink, you'll miss me!

## FACT OR FAKE?

We often hear that nothing can go faster than light, but is this true? Photons can become "entangled" with each other, so they move the same way no matter how far apart they are. This seems to break the "faster than light" law, except that nothing is actually travelling faster than light between the two photons.

## THE SCIENCE

It may be possible, in the future, to build a faster-than-light spacecraft by squashing space-time in front of it and expanding space-time behind it. This would push and pull it to superluminal speeds. It would take enormous amounts of energy, but that doesn't mean it's impossible.

### THE EXPANDING UNIVERSE

The universe itself is expanding at a speed faster than light.

**VERDICT**

**Fake**

# FROZEN WATER IS LESS DENSE THAN LIQUID WATER

## FACT OR FAKE?

Most solid objects are denser than liquids because their molecules tend to be more closely packed together. The exception is ice, which is around 9 per cent less dense than water. That's why ice floats.

## THE SCIENCE

Water is made up of one oxygen and two hydrogen atoms. When water cools, the hydrogen atoms form bonds in a hexagonal structure that keep the oxygen atoms apart. In the middle of the hexagons there's lots of empty space, which is why ice is less dense.

VERDICT
Fact

# THE WORLD'S MOST ACCURATE CLOCK IS OFF BY ONE SECOND EVERY 90 BILLION YEARS

## FACT OR FAKE?

The quantum gas atomic clock is the most accurate clock ever built. Like all atomic clocks, it measures time by using the extremely regular vibrations of atoms. The clock is located at the University of Colorado Boulder, USA.

## THE SCIENCE

The quantum gas atomic clock uses strontium atoms. Laser beams fired at the atoms keep them at an extremely chilly -273 °C. This stops them moving around and bumping into each other, which could throw out the accuracy of their vibrations.

### BETTER THAN YOUR AVERAGE STOPWATCH!

The quantum gas atomic clock can measure time down to a trillionth of a second. This could be useful for measuring extremely fast movements in nature.

**VERDICT**

*Fact*

# YOU CAN HEAR THE WIND BLOW

## FACT OR FAKE?

We've all heard the whispering wind. However, it's not the wind itself that's making this sound. What you're hearing are the sounds of air moving past or against small objects.

## THE SCIENCE

The movement of air is silent, but the friction between air and objects can cause whistling and whooshing sounds. You might be hearing the rubbing of tree branches or leaves bumping against each other, but the main thing you're hearing is the sound of the wind moving against your ears, head and body. That's why you can hear the wind blowing even when there's nothing around but you.

## VERDICT
### Fake

# PHONES USE UP ENERGY

## FACT OR FAKE?

Your phone cannot "use up" or "run out of" energy. Energy can't be gained or lost. The same amount of energy exists in the universe before and after you've used your phone – it's merely transformed from one form into another.

## THE SCIENCE

Your phone's battery contains chemical energy, which is transformed into the electrical energy of electrons moving through a circuit. Some of this transforms into light energy (for the screen) and sound energy (the noises your phone makes), as well as wasted heat energy as the phone warms with use.

**VERDICT**

**Fake**

# THE UNIVERSE IS APPROXIMATELY 13.8 BILLION YEARS OLD

*That makes me positively young!*

## FACT OR FAKE?

Scientists have estimated that the universe is 13.8 billion years old. They did this by looking for the oldest stars, since the universe cannot be any younger than its stars. Scientists worked them out to be at least 11 billion years old.

## THE SCIENCE

Another method scientists used was to measure the rate of expansion of the universe. If the expansion rate is known, scientists can work backwards to determine the time since the Big Bang, when the universe began.

### HUBBLE CONSTANT

The rate of expansion is known as the Hubble constant, named after American astronomer Edwin Hubble, who, in the 1920s, discovered the universe was expanding.

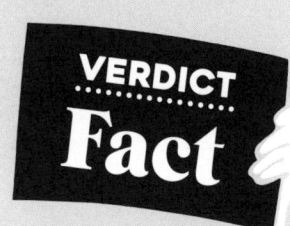

**VERDICT**

## Fact

# ATOMS
# 99.999
# EMPTY

Atoms are almost entirely empty space, and since everything's made of atoms, that means we are, too. If we got rid of all the space inside our atoms, the entire human race would fit into the volume of a sugar cube.

## THE SCIENCE

An atom is 100,000 times bigger than its nucleus, and its electrons orbit so far from the nucleus that if the nucleus was the size of a pea, the atom would be about the size of a sports arena.

# ARE 999% SPACE

## SO HOW DO WE TOUCH THINGS?

We don't actually touch anything. When you hold someone's hand you're not touching their atoms, what you're feeling is the electromagnetic force of your electrons pushing away their electrons.

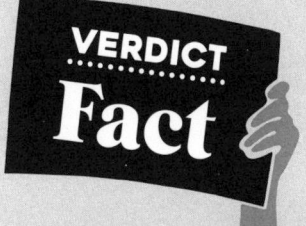

VERDICT

Fact

# YOU CAN KILL A VIRUS

## FACT OR FAKE?

Viruses aren't really alive. They don't eat, breathe or make energy. They're almost completely dependent on the cells they take over. On their own they do nothing. Therefore, it's probably not accurate to say you can kill a virus. You can deactivate it, but that's like saying you can kill a computer by unplugging it.

## THE SCIENCE

Some scientists argue that viruses are alive, but it's just a different form of life, and maybe the line between alive and not alive is more blurry than we think. There are more viruses in the world than there are cells, and probably millions of undiscovered species of virus. We still have a lot to learn about these things.

VERDICT
**Fake**
(PROBABLY)

# HUMANS CAN MAKE NEW ELEMENTS

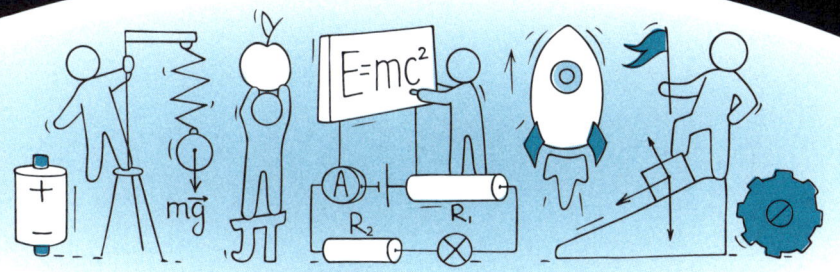

There are 118 known elements – 94 are found in nature; the rest are made in labs. New elements are unstable, and most immediately decay into other elements.

## THE SCIENCE

Each element has a unique number of protons in its atoms. Hydrogen atoms have one proton; carbon atoms have six. Scientists make artificial elements by forcing extra protons into the nucleus of an existing element. They do this in particle accelerators – machines that push particles to enormous speeds and crash them into each other.

### PLUTONIUM

In 1940, scientists bombarded a sample of the element uranium with neutrons. One neutron penetrated a uranium atom and turned into a proton, creating a new element, plutonium.

**VERDICT**
................
**Fact**

# THERE IS NO SUCH THING AS "NOW"

We split time into past, present and future. We know what the past and future are, but what exactly is the present? As soon as you sense "now", it's gone and becomes part of the past. It's a point in time with no duration, so maybe now doesn't exist.

## THE SCIENCE

You may think that "now" exists because of how we experience time. We remember the past and imagine the future, but we live in the present, don't we? Actually, we don't. Our brains take around 1/10th of a second to process what our eyes are seeing, so what we're seeing is actually the past. That's why we find it so hard to swat a fly in mid-air!

**VERDICT**
**Fact**

# THE BIG BANG
## WAS AN EXPLOSION

### THAT STARTED THE UNIVERSE

## FACT OR FAKE?

The universe is expanding, and this suggests that it began from a single point. We call this the Big Bang. The name makes you imagine an explosion, but scientists don't believe this is what happened.

## THE SCIENCE

If the Big Bang was an explosion, it would have had to happen somewhere – it would have exploded outwards into space from some central point. But the evidence from astronomers shows there's no "centre" of the universe: everything's moving away from everything else. Space is expanding in all directions equally.

## NO SPACE

A bomb explosion expands through the air, but the Big Bang expanded through nothing, because there was no space to expand into. The Big Bang created space itself to expand into.

## VERDICT
# Fake

69

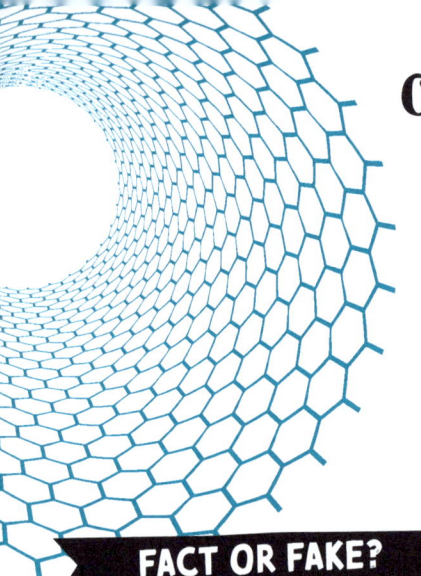

# CARBON NANOTUBES ARE THINNER THAN A HAIR AND STRONGER THAN STEEL

## THE SCIENCE

Carbon nanotubes are composed of rolled-up sheets of a single layer of carbon molecules, called graphene. As well as being light and strong, they are also very good at conducting heat and electricity. They have many potential future applications.

## FACT OR FAKE?

Carbon nanotubes are incredibly thin tubes made of carbon. They have diameters that are 50,000 times thinner than a human hair, yet, relative to their mass, they are 117 times stronger than steel.

## FUTURE USES

Carbon nanotubes may one day be used to build body armour, wind-turbine blades, algae-resistant paint, paper-thin speakers, sensors for diagnosing disease, and even elevators to space.

## VERDICT

## Fact

# TELEPORTATION IS IMPOSSIBLE

 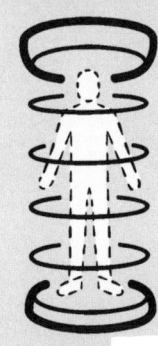 

## THE SCIENCE

Pairs of particles can become entangled (each affecting the other) even if separated across vast distances. Scientists used a pair of entangled photons to send information about a third photon. They scanned the photon, beamed the information and recreated the photon in another place. The original photon is destroyed in the process.

## FACT OR FAKE?

Teleportation – the possibility of transporting humans across space instantly – remains in the realm of science fiction. Yet scientists have managed to teleport tiny particles called photons up to a distance of 500 kilometres. This involves the transportation of information rather than matter.

**VERDICT**
········
**Fake**

# THE PRIMARY COLOURS OF LIGHT ARE RED, BLUE AND YELLOW

## FACT OR FAKE?

Painters mix red, blue and yellow to get other colours like orange and green. However, in terms of how our eyes see light, the primary colours are red, blue and green.

## THE SCIENCE

Light hits our eyes in different wavelengths, which we see as colours. At the backs of our eyes are special light-sensitive cones. One set is sensitive to red light, another to green light, and a third to blue light. Our brain converts this information into the full range of colours that we see.

### PRINTING COLOURS

Printers use a different set of primary colours to achieve the range of colours we see in books and posters. These are cyan, magenta and yellow.

**VERDICT**
.............
**Fake**

# GOLD CAN BE MADE SO THIN THAT IT APPEARS TRANSPARENT

Bling!

## FACT OR FAKE?

Gold is the most malleable of all the metals. It can be beaten to a thickness of just 0.05 microns. In other words, 2,000 of these gold sheets would be as thick as a single sheet of paper. At this thickness, gold is transparent. It can be used, for example, to coat the visors of space helmets. The gold layer reduces glare and heat from sunlight.

## THE SCIENCE

Gold is more malleable than other metals because its atoms slide past each other relatively easily. By contrast, tungsten is very hard and brittle, because its atoms are tightly linked.

**VERDICT**

## Fact

# ISAAC NEWTON DISCOVERED GRAVITY WHEN AN APPLE FELL ON HIS HEAD

## FACT OR FAKE?

The story goes that an apple fell on Newton's head and suddenly he understood gravity. It didn't quite happen like that. According to Newton, he saw an apple fall and thought: why does it fall straight down? This thought led him to develop his theory of gravity.

## THE SCIENCE

Newton was the first scientist to understand that gravity applied to all objects from an apple to the Moon.

**VERDICT**
............
**Fake**

## APPLES, CANNONBALLS AND MOONS

Newton compared the straight drop of an apple to the curved drop of a cannonball. He realised that if the cannonball went fast enough it wouldn't ever drop to Earth but "fall around it" forever. It would be in orbit around Earth like the Moon!

# SOUND TRAVELS FASTER THROUGH WATER AND STEEL THAN IT DOES THROUGH AIR

## FACT OR FAKE?

You would expect sound to travel fastest through gas, then liquid, then solid. In fact, the reverse is true. Sound travels well over four times faster in water, and over 17 times faster through steel, than it does through air.

## THE SCIENCE

Sound moves by vibrating molecules of matter. It travels faster through liquids because the molecules are closer together so there are more molecules to vibrate. In solids, the molecules are even more densely packed, so sound travels faster still.

### HOT MEANS QUICK

The speed of sound is also affected by temperature. On hot days, sound travels faster because air molecules are jiggling around and bumping into each other more.

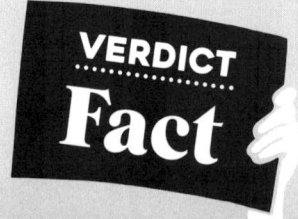

## VERDICT
### Fact

# LIGHT CAN BE BOTH A WAVE AND A PARTICLE

## FACT OR FAKE?

In 1803, British scientist Thomas Young shone a light through two slits. The pattern on the wall behind showed the rays passing through each other like colliding waves on a shore. In 1905, Albert Einstein showed that if you shone light on a metal, you could knock electrons out of it, as if light was made of particles (these were later called photons). Light sometimes acts like a wave and sometimes like a particle.

## THE SCIENCE

Light spreads through space like a wave, yet when it strikes matter, it behaves like a particle, depositing all its energy at a single point. It's as if a wave, on meeting a surfer, dumped all its energy on her, while the rest of the wave disappears.

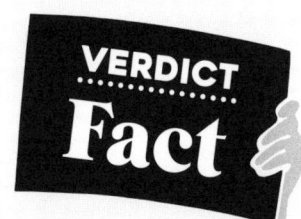

VERDICT

**Fact**

# ONLY SHINY SURFACES REFLECT LIGHT

## FACT OR FAKE?

You might think only shiny surfaces like mirrors, water or polished metal reflect light. In fact, light reflects off all surfaces, but the way it reflects is different.

**VERDICT**
## Fake

## THE SCIENCE

When light reflects off a smooth, shiny surface, it will bounce back at the same angle as it struck the surface. It appears shiny because so much light is coming back in one direction. This is called specular reflection. When light hits a rough surface, it reflects back in lots of different directions. This is called diffuse reflection.

# AN OBJECT THAT'S NOT MOVING HAS NO ENERGY

## FACT OR FAKE?

We think of a wave or a speeding bullet as having energy, but things can have energy even if they're not moving. A drawn bow about to release its arrow has energy. So does a hammer poised to strike a nail or a parked car full of fuel. Scientists call this potential energy.

## THE SCIENCE

An object has potential energy if there's tension inside it (think of a stretched elastic band) or because of its position in relation to other objects (like a boulder ready to roll off a cliff).

### KINETIC ENERGY

When you release the arrow, potential energy is changed into kinetic energy (the energy of a body in motion).

**VERDICT**

**Fake**

# HEAT ALWAYS RISES

Heat doesn't only rise. It can move in any direction. Hot air rises, but heat and hot air are not the same thing.

## THE SCIENCE

Heat travels in three ways: 1. Hot objects can emit heat in the form of waves of energy (thermal radiation) that heat up the objects they hit. 2. If a hot object comes into contact with another object, heat can pass through the touching surface (conduction). 3. If a hot object touches air or water, it can be carried to new places (convection). If it touches air, the hot air will rise, though not immediately, as you'll know if you stand next to a fire.

VERDICT
Fake

# IT CAN TAKE UP TO 1000 YEARS FOR PLASTIC TO DECOMPOSE

## FACT OR FAKE?

Materials decompose at different speeds. Orange peel takes six months; milk cartons take five years. Plastic takes up to 1000 years, which is why plastic waste is causing a pollution crisis on our planet.

## THE SCIENCE

Most waste is broken down by bacteria, but very few bacteria can break down plastic. Plastic decomposes through exposure to sunlight – ultraviolet rays from the Sun break the bonds holding plastic's long molecular chains together – but this can take centuries.

### PLASTIC-EATER

Scientists have discovered a bacterium that produces enzymes that enable it to eat plastic. By creating better, faster forms of these enzymes in the lab, scientists may be able to help beat the plague of plastic waste.

## VERDICT
# Fact

# PLASTIC CAN STOP BULLETS AND KNIVES

Kevlar is a plastic material used to make bulletproof vests and body armour. It's stronger than steel, but about five and a half times less dense, which is why it's light and flexible to wear – unlike the suits of armour worn by medieval knights!

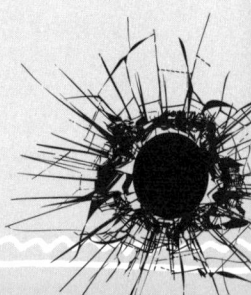

## THE SCIENCE

Kevlar's chemical structure is made up of lots of straight rods bonded together. The basic material is spun into tightly woven plastic fibres that are extremely hard to move apart. A bullet hitting Kevlar will lose all or most of its energy fighting its way through the material.

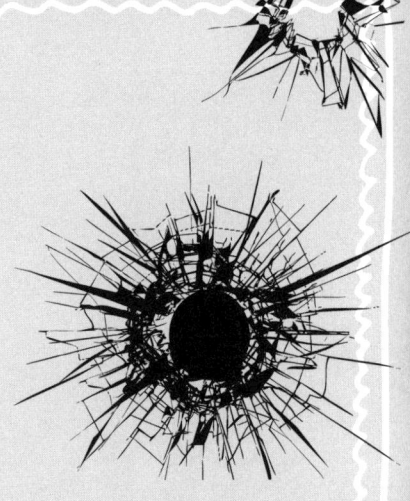

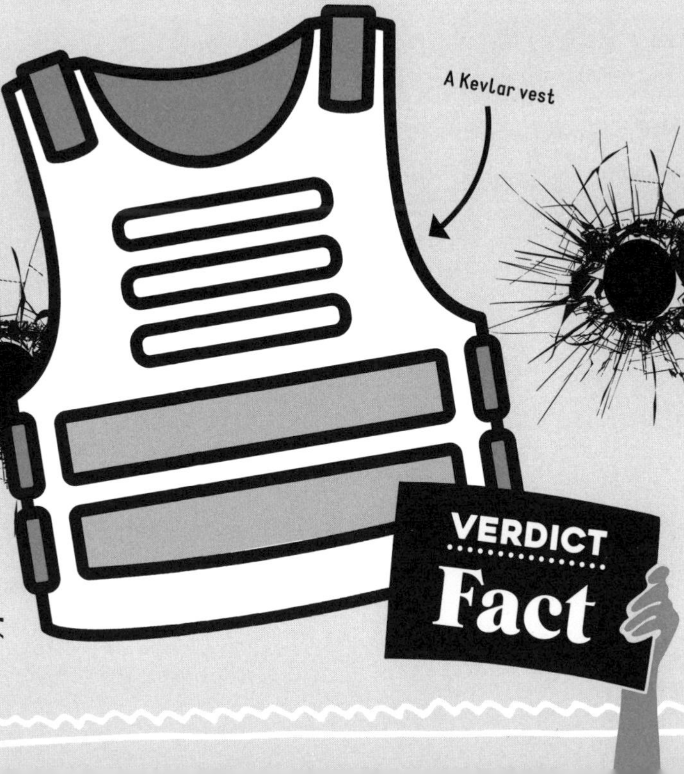

A Kevlar vest

VERDICT
Fact

# MAGNETISM IS STRONGER THAN GRAVITY

It's often said that magnetism is stronger than gravity. It's true that the smallest magnet can pick up a paperclip from the floor, so magnetism is stronger than gravity in that situation, but that doesn't mean it's stronger in all situations.

## THE SCIENCE

Gravity is far weaker than magnetism at small scales, but at the scale of stars and planets, it's a lot stronger. That's because as objects get further apart, the gravity between them decreases at a slower rate than does their magnetic attraction.

### VERDICT
## Fake

### DECREASING WITH DISTANCE

Double the distance between two objects, gravity decreases by four times, but magnetism decreases by 16 times.

84

# THE HOTTEST TEMPERATURE RECORDED ON EARTH IS HOTTER THAN THE CENTRE OF THE SUN

## FACT OR FAKE?

In 2012, scientists at the Large Hadron Collider in Geneva briefly created temperatures of 5.5 trillion °C. That's way hotter than the centre of the sun, which is 15 million °C.

## THE SCIENCE

Scientists did this by smashing together atoms at 99 per cent of the speed of light. They were trying to create a quark-gluon plasma – a form of matter that existed just after the Big Bang. In these first few microseconds after the universe's birth, things were so hot that atoms couldn't exist, and it was filled with miniscule particles called quarks and gluons.

## VERDICT
## Fact

# ANTIMATTER COULD HAVE DESTROYED THE UNIVERSE AT BIRTH

## FACT OR FAKE?

Antimatter sounds like science fiction, but it's real. When antimatter and matter meet, they destroy each other. During the Big Bang, matter and antimatter were created in equal quantities, so the universe could have been destroyed. Scientists are still trying to work out why it wasn't. Some suggest that slightly more matter than antimatter was created, which is why matter won out.

## THE SCIENCE

Every kind of particle has its own antimatter particle, which is almost identical but has the opposite electrical charge. So an electron has a negative charge, but its antiparticle, the positron, has a positive charge. Antiparticles are rare but are briefly produced when, for example, cosmic rays hit Earth's atmosphere.

**VERDICT**

*Fact*

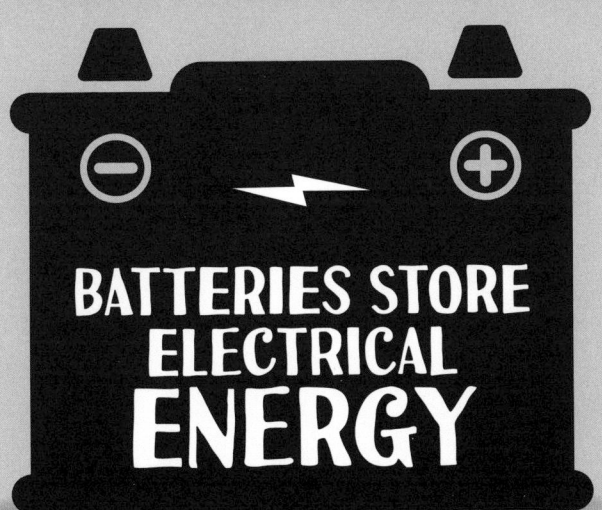

# BATTERIES STORE ELECTRICAL ENERGY

## FACT OR FAKE?

A battery produces electricity, but it doesn't store electrical energy. It stores chemical energy, which it converts into electrical energy.

### FLAT BATTERY

As the electrons flow from anode to cathode, chemical products gradually form, creating resistance. As resistance builds, the chemical reactions slow down and the electrons stop flowing, which is how you get a flat battery.

## THE SCIENCE

A battery consists of a positive electrode (cathode) and a negative electrode (anode) separated by a liquid called an electrolyte that conducts electricity. The energy is stored in the materials of these three components. When the battery is used, the electrodes react chemically with the electrolyte, causing a flow of electrons from the anode to the cathode, providing electrical energy.

## VERDICT
Fake

# BLACK HOLES GLOW

## FACT OR FAKE?

A black hole is a region in space of crushing pressures. You'd think nothing could escape its gravitational pull. And yet, in 1974, English scientist Stephen Hawking discovered that black holes emit radiation.

## THE SCIENCE

At the edge of a black hole, gravity is so intense that particle pairs (see panel) won't always destroy each other. Before they can do so, the negative particle may fall into the black hole while the positive particle escapes. That's how black holes radiate.

### PARTICLE PAIRS

At the level of the very small, space is never empty. Even in a vacuum, pairs of particles are continually popping into existence, one with positive energy, the other with negative energy. Almost instantly, they destroy each other.

**VERDICT**

*Fact*

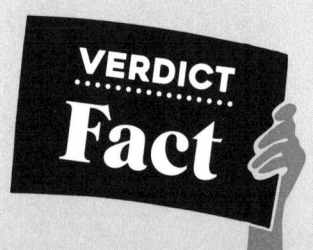

# ADDING SALT TO WATER LOWERS ITS BOILING POINT

## FACT OR FAKE?

Adding salt to a pan of water will make it boil slightly faster, but this isn't because salt lowers the water's boiling point. It just means that less heat is needed for saltwater to reach boiling point than for freshwater.

## THE SCIENCE

Adding salt actually raises the boiling point of water because it makes it harder for water molecules to escape from the pan as steam. We don't notice this because the temperature rises more quickly.

VERDICT

Fake

# IT'S OKAY TO EAT DROPPED FOOD IF YOU PICK IT UP WITHIN FIVE SECONDS

It's known as the five-second rule. Somehow we convince ourselves that germs can't find their way onto our dropped sandwich if we pick it up within five seconds. Sadly, the five-second rule is completely fake!

## THE SCIENCE

Scientists have tested the rule and found that bacteria can attach themselves to dropped food even if it's picked up really fast. It's true that the longer food spends on the floor, the more germs it will pick up, and foods with wet surfaces, like an orange slice, can pick up bacteria more easily. But as a general rule, do not eat food that's been on the floor.

VERDICT
..............
**Fake**

# SCIENCE IS A COLLECTION OF FACTS

It's easy to imagine science as a body of knowledge contained on websites and in books and that to master the subject one only needs to read all this material. Yet science is so much more than a collection of facts.

## THE SCIENCE

Science is a process that will never be complete. It's exciting and dynamic. Every day, new discoveries are being made that are changing or refining our knowledge of the universe. To be a scientist is only partly about learning facts; it's also about asking questions, collecting data, coming up with theories and testing them in experiments.

VERDICT
**Fake**

# GLOSSARY

**air resistance** – a force in air that impedes movement through it

**alkali metals** – a group of metals that are all shiny, soft and highly reactive

**atmosphere** – the layer of gases that surrounds a very large object, such as a planet or star

**atmospheric pressure** – the pressure exerted by the weight of the atmosphere

**atom** – the smallest particle of a chemical element

**bacteria** (singular bacterium) – single-celled microscopic organisms, some of which cause diseases

**Big Bang** – the rapid expansion of space from a state of extreme temperature and pressure, which scientists believe marked the beginning of the universe

**condensation** – the conversion of vapour or gas into liquid

**conduct** – transmit (electricity or heat)

**cosmic ray** – a highly energetic particle travelling through space at close to the speed of light

**crystal** – a solid consisting of a symmetrical, ordered arrangement of atoms or molecules

**decompose** – break down into smaller, simpler parts

**density** – the compactness of a substance

**discharge** – the release or outflow of something, such as electricity

**electric charge** – the electrical quality of an object. Electric charges can be positive or negative

**electric field** – the area that surrounds an electrically charged particle where it can exert force on other charged particles within the field

**electricity** – a form of energy resulting from the existence of charged particles such as electrons or protons

**electrode** – a conductor through which electricity enters or leaves an object

**electrolyte** – a substance that contains ions and conducts electricity

**electromagnet** – a magnet produced by winding a coil of wire around a core of iron and passing an electric current through the wire. Unlike permanent magnets, the magnetic field of an electromagnet can be changed by controlling the electric current running through it

**electromagnetism** – the interaction of electric and magnetic fields

**electromagnetic spectrum** – the range of wavelengths of different forms of radiation, such as gamma waves, X-rays, light waves, microwaves and radio waves

**electron** – a particle with a negative electric charge. Electrons are found in all atoms and they carry electricity through solids

**enzyme** – a chemical substance produced by a living organism that speeds up (or slows down) a chemical reaction, such as digesting food

**equator** – an imaginary line drawn around the middle of Earth, equally distant from both poles and dividing Earth into northern and southern hemispheres

**evaporate** – change from liquid into gas or vapour

**friction** – the resistance an object encounters when moving over or through some form of matter

**gravity** – the force of attraction between two objects, its strength depending on the mass of the objects

**hemisphere** – one-half of a ball-shaped or spherical object, such as the Earth

**humidity** – atmospheric moisture

**inertia** – the tendency of an object to continue at rest or in motion going in a straight line unless acted upon by an external force

**insulator** – a substance that does not (or does not easily) conduct electricity

**ion** – an atom with an electric charge (either positive or negative) due to the loss or gain of one or more electrons

**magnetic field** – the region around a magnet within which the magnetic force acts

**malleable** – (of a material) able to be beaten or pressed into shape without breaking or cracking

**mantle** – the region of Earth between the crust and the core believed to consist of dense, semi-molten rocks

**mass** – the amount of matter in an object

**microwave** – an electromagnetic wave with a wavelength shorter than a radio wave but longer than infrared radiation

**molecule** – two or more atoms joined or bonded together

**momentum** – the amount of motion of a moving object, which can be measured by adding its mass to its velocity

**neutron** – a particle with no electric charge, found in the nuclei of all atoms except hydrogen.

**nucleus** – the central core of an atom, consisting of protons and neutrons and carrying a positive electric charge

**particle** – any of the subatomic (smaller than an atom) constituents of the physical world, including electrons, photons and protons

# GLOSSARY

**photon** – a particle of light or some other form of electromagnetic radiation

**plasma** – a gas consisting of positive ions, formed at very high temperatures and found in stars

**proton** – a particle with a positive electric charge, found in the nuclei of all atoms

**radiation** – giving out or emitting energy, usually as waves or particles, such as light, heat and sound

**radioactive** – radiation with enough energy to ionize atoms or molecules (strip them of electrons)

**refract** – make (a ray of light) change direction. Water, air or glass can refract rays of light

**sound barrier** – the increased air resistance and other effects that occur when an object approaches the speed of sound

**space-time** – time and the three dimensions of space considered as one four-dimensional structure

**static electricity** – an electric charge, often produced by friction, which causes sparks or crackling or the attraction of dust or hair

**superluminal** – having a speed greater than light

**surface tension** – a skin-like tension at the surface of a liquid caused by strong bonds between the surface molecules and the ones below

**ultraviolet (UV)** – a type of electrical and magnetic energy with waves shorter than light waves but longer than X-rays

**vacuum** – a totally empty space, containing no objects or matter

**vapour** – the gaseous form of a substance that may be above or just below its boiling point

**virus** – a tiny parasite that can only reproduce inside a host cell

**wavelength** – the distance between the peak (or crest) of one wave and the next, for example, in light or sound waves

**weight** – the force exerted on the mass of a body by gravity

# FURTHER INFORMATION

## BOOKS

**Science (Go Quiz Yourself)**
by Izzi Howell, Wayland, 2020

**Science Skills Sorted (series)**
by Anna Claybourne and Angela Royston,
Franklin Watts, 2018-20

**Super Smart Science (series)**
by Dr Matthew Bluteua, Dr Alistair Butcher
and Dr Vincent Tobin, Wayland, 2021

## WEBSITES

**www.bbc.co.uk/bitesize/subjects/z2pfb9q**
This website contains information, games, videos and quizzes
about science.

**www.natgeokids.com/uk/category/discover/science**
If you love amazing facts about science, this is the website for
you. You'll find out things you never knew on subjects like space
junk, jellyfish, tomatoes and the human brain.

**wowscience.co.uk**
This is a huge collection of games, activities, videos and
experiments on every science subject you can think of.

# INDEX